D0961545

That's Not How We Do It Here!

658.406 K848T 2016
John Kotter
That's Not How We Do It Here

That's Not How We Do It Here!

A Story About How Organizations Rise,
Fall—and Can Rise Again

John Kotter
Holger Rathgeber

PORTFOLIO/PENGUIN

PORTFOLIO / PENGUIN
An imprint of Penguin Random House LLC
375 Hudson Street
New York, New York 10014

Copyright © 2016 by John Kotter and Holger Rathgeber
Penguin supports copyright. Copyright fuels creativity, encourages diverse voices, promotes free speech, and creates a vibrant culture. Thank you for buying an authorized edition of this book and for complying with copyright laws by not reproducing, scanning, or distributing any part of it in any form without permission. You are supporting writers and allowing Penguin to continue to publish books for every reader.

Illustrations by Kari Fry. Copyright © 2016 by Kotter Associates.

ISBN 9780399563942
E-book ISBN 9780399563959

Printed in the United States of America
1   3   5   7   9   10   8   6   4   2

Designed by Cassandra Garruzzo

That's Not How We Do It Here! is available at a discount when purchased in quantity for sales promotions or corporate use. Special editions, which include personalized covers, excerpts, and corporate imprints, can be created when purchased in large quantities. For more information, please call 212-572-2232 or e-mail specialmarkets@penguinrandomhouse.com. Your local bookstore can also assist with discounted bulk purchases using the Penguin Random House corporate Business-to-Business program. For assistance in locating a participating retailer, e-mail B2B@penguinrandomhouse.com.

That's Not How We Do It Here!

The vultures had mysteriously turned from scavengers to killers. No one knew why. These awful, scary, deadly creatures were probably the final blow that was leading to the collapse of Matt's clan.

Matt was a Meerkat—those smallish African animals that humans seem to find cute and interesting. Matt, like all Kats, had his own distinct personality and skills. He had always been shy and could be a bit too rigid once he had a plan in mind. But an inherent sense of loyalty, a soft smile, and skills he always used to help the group had made him much appreciated. He had usually enjoyed life, and most of the time life had enjoyed him back.

But then . . .

Because the rain seemed to have disappeared, his clan of fuzzy little creatures no longer had enough food for everyone. At least once a day, Matt ate less so the young and old and weak could have more. But that hardly made even a small contribution to solving the problem. The increase in the number of predators was—well, Matt had never seen anything like it. A few Kats said it was all connected. Less rain meant less food, which was leading to strange and unpredictable changes in predator behavior. But who knew for sure?

They could not seem to agree upon, much less bring alive, any new big ideas to deal with the new problems. For Matt and many others, that was incredibly frustrating. Making matters even worse, getting the most routine daily work done was proving more and more difficult.

It was not as if Matt never heard any promising new ideas. He had two very creative friends, Tanya and Ago, who had come up with a possible way to find more food and waste less, and a potential method of spotting predators faster than before. But both Kats ran into a wall of "that's not the way we do things here," a reaction that, considering the circumstances, made no sense. Matt tried to pitch in and show others why such an argument was illogical. He talked to Kats he knew the best, those born in litters about the same time as he was. He talked to his Family Chief. And he got nowhere.

Matt was so tired. Because he was respected, he was asked by one of the big bosses—an Alpha—to take on this project and that project and another. The toll on him added up. He was not at all the type who walked through his days quietly or loudly angry at the world. Yet here he was . . .

One very mad Meerkat.

Introduction

This story is about important issues almost all of us are now facing: The rate of change is going up, that fact can be hard to see clearly or to deal with well, and when we cannot find ways to avoid hazards, grasp opportunities, and produce the results we all truly value—all of which we know is possible because some people do it—life can become quite unpleasant.

We have chosen a fable format here—a story with a whole cast of characters, including Matt—because fables can take on big issues and be useful for many people. And the issues here really are big. To understand how we can get better outcomes, we need to more clearly understand how organizations rise, why they often eventually struggle no matter their past success, and why they can fall. We need more clarity about how a few rise once again to grow, fulfill their mission, create great jobs and services and wealth. It helps to see the role that discipline, planning, reliability, and efficiency play in these stories. And the role of passion, vision, engagement, speed, agility, and culture. And there is the issue of management versus leadership—and the latter not from just a few people in big corner offices.

Yes, yes, we know that this is a bit much for a short book. And, yes, many others have had much to say about these issues. But we think there is too much fog around some fundamental points that relate to success today. Only when we begin to lift that fog do we have a chance of turning twenty-first-century challenges and threats into exciting opportunities—for our businesses, governments, nonprofits, and ourselves. We could go on and on talking about the many decades of research underlying the ideas and insights in this story. But a discussion of that here could undermine our goals of being short, thought-provoking, useful, and fun. At the end of the book we will offer some thoughts about the issues raised in that research and in the story. For now, we present only the simple diagram shown below. It has

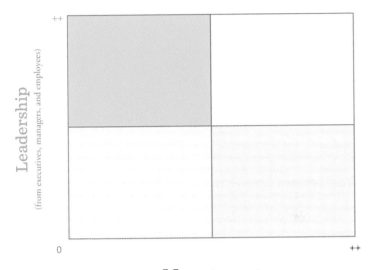

Management
(from executives, managers, and employees)

much to say about the rise and fall and possible re-rise of organizations, as well as about what each of us might do to be more effective and happier at work. We will discuss all this at the end of the book (and you will see the relevance throughout our parable).

So enough. Let's go back and start at the beginning of our story.

Chapter 1

Once upon a time there was a most interesting clan of animals that humans call Meerkats. They lived in the Kalahari, a warm and dry stretch of land in the southern part of the African continent.

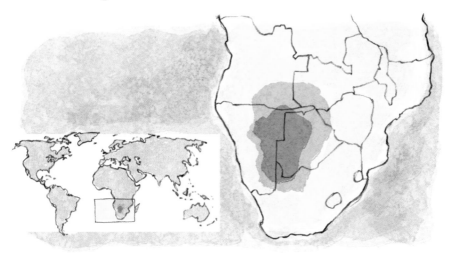

At first glance, the piece of land these Meerkats called home looked like many other areas around them. But with a mix of cleverness, hard work, hustle, and a bit of luck, their ancestors had found a place that was not like all the others. A brushfire had cleared the ground before their arrival and had created a nearly perfect habitat. Many predators had been driven away by the fire and there was plenty of food, which mostly consisted of scorpions, crunchy insects, worms, eggs, and from time to time some fruits.

The clan started with a dozen Kats and grew to more than one hundred and fifty, a remarkable size that is far from typical. Meerkats can have between two and four litters a year, with three to five pups per litter. If you do the math—well, the difference between two litters and four and between three and five little ones in each is . . . let's say that the right conditions can make a lot of additional Meerkats.

None of these conditions is more important than keeping the clan functioning well, which, as you might expect, turns out to be a more and more difficult task as it grows larger and larger. But this group had learned to manage themselves exceptionally well—which is one of the reasons their story is so interesting.

Last spring they had enjoyed good rain. Finding food was relatively easy. Life was not without its demands, but overall it was good. Everyone had his or her place, and as long as you did things the way they were supposed to be done in the clan and stayed out of trouble, things were pretty fine.

Could this change? "Of course," almost everyone would say. "Change is just a part of life. You have a dry season and then it changes to a rainy season. We have hawks trying to get us sometimes, then it changes to snakes. But we know how to deal with this. It can be tricky, but we have methods that can handle challenges like that pretty darned well, thank you."

Nadia, the Creative One

Nadia was a bright, adventurous, and energetic member of the clan. She had an outgoing personality and an enthusiasm that was infectious, especially around Meerkat children, who seemed to want to follow her everywhere. That was usually fun for her—although, as one might expect, it could occasionally be annoying.

When Nadia heard that she had to see her Family Chief at noon one day, she was understandably a little apprehensive. She had almost never had a one-on-one meeting with him.

She talked to her friends. Did they know what the meeting was about? One did. Nadia learned that she was being considered for the job of an Older Sister for a litter that would soon be able to leave its burrow.

After some thought, Nadia decided she very much wanted the job. But first she had to pass an interview with her Family Chief, who was making all appointment decisions for her group.

She was early for her meeting, so she sat down and let her mind wander.

"You are Nadia? Yes?" The Family Chief woke her up from her daydreams. He had a reputation for being tough but fair. "I have a few questions for you," he started. "First . . ."

Nadia pretty much knew all the right answers, which she gave with sufficient confidence to mask her natural nervousness. The test was hardly difficult for her, because she had in one way or another been taught those responses since she was a pup. Not all the answers made sense to her, but she figured if she wanted the job she should not try to generate a philosophical discussion on how to run a clan.

When the boss was comfortable that the young Meerkat could assume the responsibility, he asked *the* question: "Are you willing to be totally accountable for teaching your puppies what they will need to know to be adults in the clan, and for protecting their lives until they can protect themselves?"

To pass the test Nadia had about a nanosecond to say, "Yes!" And she did.

She left the meeting feeling excited, even though, to be honest, she didn't really understand much about what would be demanded of her in her new role. And that made her a bit anxious, which, again to be honest, a bright and energetic Kat was not inclined to admit to herself.

Nicholas, Disciplined and Reliable

Nicholas was Nadia's older brother and the Head of Guards. He was dedicated, thorough, detail-oriented, and very disciplined. He was also smart and handsome . . . and half of Nadia's girlfriends were quietly in love with him.

Nicholas had just finished his morning briefing with his guards. He had gone through the schedule for the day and reminded everyone of the need to be more alert than ever because of recent troubling news.

One guard had spotted a cobra in a tree close by the clan, and a jackal had also been seen wandering around. These predators would love to have a Meerkat for lunch. In both cases the guards were sure these were not the same predators that they had seen yesterday. Two jackals and two cobras at the same time was unusual. Potentially worse, another guard reported seeing something in the sky that sounded like a creature they had been told by their elders was a vulture. Since this clan had settled into its home after the brushfire, no vulture-creature had ever been seen.

Nicholas's mind was still preoccupied with what he had just heard and what he needed to do when he saw Nadia approaching him. He knew about her interview and had been sure that she would pass the test. He hugged his younger sister. She was still breathless from running and could barely speak. But after announcing she had gotten the job, she quickly noticed that something was troubling her brother. So she asked.

"Nothing special," he lied to not worry her, "just the usual work." But Nadia insisted. "What work? You are the Head of Guards, but I never see you guarding." She smiled, and Nicholas had to laugh. "No, I am not guarding. I do something else, as you well know. But do you really want to hear more about that?" he asked, sensing that a few minutes of diversion from his troubles might actually be helpful. "You have not exactly shown much interest in the past."

"Today is not the past," Nadia said with her disarming enthusiasm, sensing that this information might now be useful, given her new job. So they sat down and he explained.

"I make plans for how many guards we need and create a daily guarding schedule. We have learned over the years as our clan has grown and grown that plans and schedules are essential or some posts will accidentally go unguarded. And that can mean . . ." He shook his head. He did not have to say "dead Meerkats." Nadia understood.

"I recruit and train guards. For those who do not work out, I help find another use. Excellent guarding is a skill, and we must have it. Amateur guards? Bad idea.

"I define procedures for the guards to follow based on what we have learned over the years. I measure how often we get attacked, when, and where. We have set very aggressive goals. We do not want to fool ourselves that we are doing a good job when in fact we are not. When the clan was small, everyone could see what was happening. But not now.

"And if there is a problem with guarding, it's my responsibility to find it quickly, analyze it, and solve it. If I am slow . . ." He again shook his head.

Nadia tried to look interested, but plans, schedules, procedures, measures, and the like sounded, well . . . boring. Nicholas saw that she was struggling with something, and he still had some time before his next meeting, so he continued.

"See, to have a clan like ours function reliably, you foremost need discipline and order," he said while drawing some boxes and lines in the sand.

"Good organization is essential. That starts with our two Alphas at the top." One male and one female, as in all Meerkat clans.

"They make all the important decisions for us. Underneath you have the Betas"—six Family Chiefs each overseeing groups of twenty to thirty, along the Head of Burrows and Nicholas, Head of Guards. "Together we make sure that all the work that is necessary gets done and everyone in the clan knows what to do, when, and how."

Nicholas explained that in the recent past they had been attacked ten times every full-moon-to-full-moon cycle. He showed her how he kept track of this with twigs organized a certain way in one of their burrows. Nadia was impressed. "We have a hit rate of less than one in twenty," Nicholas said with some pride in his voice, and rightly so since for Meerkat clans that was an exceptionally good number.

Nadia, being unfamiliar with Meerkat-management jargon, asked, "What exactly is a hit rate?" Nicholas nodded. "This is how often a clan member is taken or seriously injured by a predator in relation to the total number of attacks. Of course, we do everything we can to keep it as low as possible. That is how we measure our work as guards."

Nadia couldn't help but be *very* impressed with her favorite brother, though she found the idea of sitting around and measuring this or that rather . . . uninspiring.

Nicholas drew another box underneath a Family Chief. "This is now where you fit as an Older Sister," he explained with a smile. He drew five boxes underneath. "And these are your puppies."

Nadia had two immediate reactions. First, she did not like her name put in a box, although she understood that her promotion put her in that box. Second, she did not understand why puppies would be on this chart.

"But the puppies do not work," she protested.

"Wrong," said Nicholas. "They do. Their work is to

learn to survive. Your work is to teach the puppies to succeed."

He looked at the sun and his shadow—essentially a Meerkat watch—and said, "But now I have to run for another gathering, little sister. I am proud of you." They hugged each other and he was off.

Meanwhile, Nicholas thought about a vulture, a creature he had heard about since childhood—not as a real being, for no one had seen one, but more as human children might hear of witches, goblins, and dragons.

"You First Learn the Rules, Then . . ."

Nadia was not sure what to expect in the Older Sister training sessions. She was eager to learn, more or less, because if she was to do the job, she wanted to do it well. Certainly that would be Nicholas's attitude.

When she arrived for training, her Family Chief was there. "Today we go through the rules for Older Sisters and Brothers," he said, and started immediately to go over all twenty-five of them.

Nadia was asked to repeat the rules and got twelve correct the first time. "Not bad for a start," the Chief said in his usual dry way, although in fact he was impressed by his new student.

The rest of the morning, they went over rules, back and forth, until Nadia was able to memorize most of them. "What is rule number five?" asked the Chief. "Never leave the puppies alone!" "Good. What is rule number fourteen?" "Start and end each day with a sand shower!" "Good."

"Enough for today," concluded the Chief. But Nadia

asked, "On number six: Treat all puppies the same. Why is that good?"

The Chief stood up, ready to leave, and answered, "Because it will produce the best results. If we have time I will explain later. See you tomorrow at the same time. Noon."

The rest of the training days were like the first. It was quite exhausting for a creative and adventurous mind. And the answer to Nadia's occasional why-questions was remarkably consistent too: "Because experience has shown it will produce the best results!" Although Nadia knew this answer was probably true, it did not feel very satisfying to her.

After Nadia had been able to remember again without fail all the rules correctly, she asked with some hope in her voice whether the training was completed. "No" was the short and unambiguous answer. "These were just the rules. Now you have to learn and practice the procedures."

When her teacher saw that Nadia was struggling, he explained, "The rules are just telling you *what* to do, but not *how* to do it. For most rules we have learned how to perform the task in the best way." From the tone of his voice, you might think that next to his wife, rules and procedures were his greatest love.

Nadia took a deep breath and nodded tentatively. The Chief saw it and his right foot began to thump, thump, thump on the hard, dry ground. It was the first time he became a bit impatient with his new student.

"Okay." He sighed. "What is rule number fourteen?"

"Start and end each day with a sand shower!" Nadia responded like a pistol shot.

"Good, but how do you do a sand shower?"

"Well, I would . . ." She thought for a moment. Then she explained her version of how she would have the puppies do it.

The Chief interrupted her. "Pretty close, but not exactly the way sand showers are done the best way. Let me explain. You begin with . . ."

And explain he did. Experience had shown that one way worked the best. So that was how they did it.

The monologue ended with "Clear?" "Very clear!" was

the expected answer, and Nadia heard herself saying it.

"And if I have an idea on how to improve our way of doing this, can I just try it out?" Nadia asked.

"Well, no," the Chief said cautiously. "We have an

Older Sisters and Brothers Rules and Procedures group." Even as he spoke, he knew that this might sound to Nadia rather slow and cumbersome. "They meet every month to go over the rules and procedures and talk about ideas and suggestions to improve them. Improvement is good and necessary! Obviously. But . . . you can't just say, 'Try whatever you think would be better,' for many reasons."

Nadia waited.

With foot thumping, the Family Chief continued. "Consider this. How would you feel if you tried something that seemed better and one of your puppies was hurt." His eyebrows went up. "It has happened."

Of course Nadia was horrified by the thought of accidentally hurting a puppy.

"Enough for now," her teacher said. "See you tomorrow."

He left behind a Nadia who felt both good and bad. Good: she was making progress and would certainly be able to learn all these rules and procedures and best practices easily. Bad: something in her heart was beginning to rebel and her enthusiasm about her new role was dropping from 100 to 80 to 60. Before it hit 40, she felt she needed to speak again to Nicholas.

They had had one or two conversations before where she would wonder aloud about the need for things like boxes, plans, measures, rules, procedures, and the like. Then Nicholas would smile, much more in a loving than a condescending way, and ask how life was in the clan. That was the conversation killer, because the answer was that life was very good. So if the clan prospered, maybe the thing Nicholas called "Kat-management" was really useful and needed.

"How are you progressing with your studies?" Nicholas looked at Nadia and needed no answer. "You don't like all the rules?" he asked.

"I know they are necessary. I am not stupid. But they seem so"—Nadia was searching for the right word—"limiting!" Then: "Where is the fun and excitement to play around and try out and learn new things?"

Nicholas thought for a moment before he responded. "Sometimes there are more important matters than fun and creativity, Nadia. These rules and procedures are there to help you to achieve what you and the clan care most about." After an intentional pause, he continued. "To have your puppies learn and survive and to prepare them to succeed in a tough world."

That evening Nadia's head cleared up. She wanted to do her new job well. No, actually, *very* well. And if the rules, procedures, and all the rest were what was required, she would accept them.

Her teacher noticed the change instantly the following day. Nadia stopped asking all these why-questions and instead memorized and practiced what she was told faster and better than any trainee ever had before. A few days later, the Family Chief reported to the Alphas that Nadia would soon be ready to take on her new role.

Meanwhile, she now began to see the clan with different eyes. Nadia watched more closely Meerkats cleaning burrows, digging new channels, guarding, feeding the puppies, keeping the meeting courts tidy, hunting, tending to the ill or injured, and settling little disputes. For all of her life, she had taken this for granted, even as the clan grew and grew and the work must have become much more complex. She now thought that it was actually astonishing that all this happened so well, day after day, week after week. The message from her brother, she now realized, was that the plans, lines, boxes, procedures, and other things he called management made this all happen. Or so he said. If true—and she was at least beginning to believe it was—then this management thing was actually quite amazing. Or at least it had the potential to be.

Nevertheless, the creative part of Nadia wondered if something was wrong here—or at least missing.

Chapter 2

Nadia was on her way back to her family group when she heard the alarm. Instinctively, she looked all around and saw . . . nothing. Then she sensed a shadow and looked up.

The flying creature was big, ugly, and moving at incredible speed.

Two young puppies were playing next to her with a butterfly, completely immersed in their game. Nadia grabbed them and dragged them into a burrow that was close enough for them to be safe.

Lying in the burrow, she heard screams, terrible screams. She heard the sounds of Kat-feet running. But then it all seemed to stop as quickly as it started.

She ventured out of the tunnel cautiously, keeping the pups safely behind her. The scene she found was unlike any she had witnessed before.

Those near the attack were traumatized. Those who had not seen the vulture—most of the Meerkats, since the bird had come and gone so swiftly—were struggling to understand what had happened.

Within an hour, the Alphas, named Moro and Mara, had organized a meeting. Mara, the more emotional of the two, was furious.

"How Could This Happen!!??"

Mara screamed at the six Family Chiefs, the Head of Guards, and the Head of Burrows. The vulture attack had hit two families. At least one Kat seemed to be missing, and two others were injured.

No one was inclined to speak up first. Mara broke the silence. "Protecting the clan is your first priority!" she yelled while staring at the two Family Chiefs who had been hit.

After a noticeable pause, one Family Chief finally said, "We did all we could, but there was simply not enough time between the alarm and the attack." He turned his head and stared at the Head of Guards.

All eyes shifted to Nicholas. He told them, truthfully, "According to the closest guard on duty, the time between the alarm and the attack was in line with our agreed minimum standards." He then looked at the Head of Burrows. "Did we have enough burrows in the attack zone?"

All eyes followed Nicholas's lead. The Head of Burrows blinked and looked back at the others. Then his expression hardened.

"Well, I cannot judge how reliable the report of the guard on duty really is." He paused. "But my diggers confirmed that all burrows were cared for properly and accessible."

Eyes seemed to automatically, and in unison, go to the second Family Chief, whose expression had already shifted from confusion and sadness to the preparation of a defense—which did not impress Mara one bit. Her face turned as red as a Meerkat face could ever become. "*This is unacceptable!*" she screamed as she abruptly closed the meeting and scheduled another session for later in the day.

Meanwhile, Nadia was distraught. She kept thinking about the puppies, and her emotions showed. Nicholas was distraught too, but he had long ago learned that in his job he should not show it. He should act. So even before the Alphas started to have additional meetings, Nicholas sprang into action.

He assigned two of his guards the task of finding a

way to reduce their response time. He assigned two others to find ways to do everything more efficiently so they could free up resources to create one or, ideally, two more lookout locations. He took it upon himself to decide where best to place new guards.

One fellow Beta also reacted quickly, and in a similar way. Two others seemed to spend most of their time coming up with reasons for why the problems were not their fault.

Over the next days and weeks the number of vulture attacks increased. And as if that were not enough, the rain was late.

Meerkats do not need to drink much at all as long as they have juicy insects and reptiles to devour. But finding this water-filled food becomes harder, much harder, when the rain is late. The little creatures Meerkats need to survive dig themselves deeper and deeper into the soil to find moisture. And they stop any activity that requires energy but is not urgent under those circumstances. Activities like . . . reproduction. Which means both less food and less water for the Meerkats.

The stress level in the clan went way up. The Alpha/ Beta meetings became painful. Mara kept demanding more and more information on the water and food supply problems. But no one had all this information or the time to look for it. This didn't lift Mara's mood.

"I want a proposal of how we will measure food supply and consumption levels in the future," she growled in Meerkat-management-speak. She pointed to three Family Chiefs: "Can I have it for our next meeting?" The

Betas had been around long enough to know that the right and only answer under the circumstances was, "Of course."

Nicholas hated that they did not seem to be making the necessary progress. Certainly a bit more cooperation among the Alphas and Betas and less time spent on figuring out who was to blame would help. But even then . . . A little of this was just Meerkat-nature, he thought. So he worked even harder.

After a few nights without enough sleep, Nicholas began to feel less than his normal strong and confident self.

Nadia, in addition to thinking about her pups, and what she needed to do that day or that hour, found herself thinking about bigger questions. Where would a vulture suddenly come from? No one knew. It was fast and able to cover a lot of ground in a very short period of time, she thought. Had the drought driven it to expand its hunting zone? And a troubling thought was growing and weighing on her as she connected the dots. If that was true, a vulture might be just the first new threat showing up. Would more predators soon follow?

Guarding from the Top of a Tree

Ayo had always wanted to be a guard, a great guard, when Nicholas recruited him a year ago. Some of his friends saw it as a duty or something they had to do as a member of the clan. For Ayo it was much more. When he was guarding, he was 100 percent focused on the work. When he was not guarding, he was thinking about guarding and ways of doing it not just well, but with perfection. He couldn't help it. He was a guard-nerd.

As Ayo was returning from his guarding post, he ran into his very best friend, Nadia. They had loved to spend time together ever since they were puppies, even though they were in some ways quite different—Nadia so outgoing and with wide curiosity and interests, Ayo so focused and, let us say, without the best social skills.

Ayo said in his typically intense and somewhat abrupt manner, "Come, let me show you something," and dragged her forward. Although her mind was distracted by the confusion and crises, she still went with him without question or comment.

They came to the largest tree around. "Let's go up," he said as he jumped onto the tree, digging his sharp claws into the bark and pulling his body up a few feet.

"I can't climb a tree," said Nadia.

"And how do you know?" asked Ayo.

"I have never done it," said Nadia, immediately realizing how little sense her answer made.

A few minutes later, they were some thirty feet off the ground. "I am not going any farther," Nadia announced firmly.

"You don't have to. Look around!" said Ayo.

They were sitting near each other on thick branches overlooking the vast territory.

"Wow," Nadia couldn't help but say. This was the most amazing thing she had done and seen in a long time.

For the next thirty minutes Ayo talked relentlessly about how they could revolutionize guarding. "From

up here you can see danger more quickly than from the ground, which gives us more time to react. You can see that horrible vulture coming at us much sooner! Yes?"

Yes indeed, Nadia thought to herself. This was a great idea. They had to talk to Nicholas.

Meeting, Measuring, Task Forces, Policies, Staffing, Planning...

The Alphas spent more time meeting with each other than ever before. They had long chats between themselves about some Betas who they believed were not up to the job. Then about who was ready to replace those Meerkats. And how they could best deal with the inevitable drama of delivering bad news to the unqualified.

The Alphas met each morning and afternoon with the Betas. Among other actions they decided upon were to:

- Review their method of dealing with snake attacks. The current process, developed over the years, had seven steps. After a two-hour discussion about the second half of the fourth step, the Meerkat equivalent of a task force was created and asked to finish the work.
- Review the very structure of how they organized themselves. Two Family Chiefs argued (logically) for eliminating the guarding and burrow-

ing units and folding those tasks into the family units. The Head of Burrows suggested, instead, that burrows and guarding should be consolidated under him.

- Discuss further their first version of a new set of measures for catching and consuming food. The latest proposal made a lot of sense but required twenty-three measures.

- Examine the new training plan for the whole clan to (re)learn/practice the four alarm signals and appropriate actions.

	Low Alert	High Alert
Ground Attack	Signal 1	Signal 2
Air Attack	Signal 3	Signal 4

When they were not meeting, the bosses, driven more by Mara than Moro, did more commanding and controlling than they had ever done before. And why not? Mara had more experience than anyone. She knew more. So she told, told, told—or more likely yelled, yelled, yelled. She put a lot of pressure on herself, didn't rest, and expected no less from others. One consequence was that the Betas and many in the clan became increasingly stressed out. Their jobs had suddenly become not only demanding but also exhausting.

The clan speculated on what the bosses were meeting about all the time. Those who worried easily and those who never trusted their superiors spread all sorts of inaccurate news in the absence of clear communication from above. Any broader strategy the Alphas had was truly understood by no more than a half dozen other Kats.

Then additional consequences of the growing food problem made life even worse.

Meerkats look like they go daily to a gym. They have no fat. The good news: Because of their genetic makeup they do not need to suffer in a Kalahari Health Club and yet will never have an ounce of chubbiness to carry around. Not so good: They cannot build any fat reserves at all, so a single day without food is a problem, two days without food is a serious problem, and three days without food can be fatal. With finding enough food an increasing challenge, more and more Meerkats began to take care of only themselves. The stronger stole from the weaker. When the Alphas heard about this, they ordered the Betas to stop their families, their guards, or their burrow-makers from letting the clan fall into a vicious survival-of-the-fittest mode. Lectures from Betas to others had some effect, but did not eliminate the problem. Desperate Meerkats were simply more discreet in their self-protective actions.

The Final Straw

Ayo climbed down the tree from where he had been doing all his guarding. His shift was over and his replacement had arrived. "Nicholas wants to see you," the replacement told him.

Finally! Ayo thought. He had been desperately trying to speak with his boss to explain what he had discovered, but Nicholas seemed always to be in meetings, talking to other Betas, or distracted. Although Ayo hadn't eaten for the whole day, he felt excited. Now he could explain his idea to Nicholas.

Before Ayo could open his mouth, a cold, weary, and unfriendly-looking Nicholas firmly said, "Ayo, I have received a report from other guards that you have violated guarding procedures. Is it true that you have climbed a tree while on post?"

Ayo did not let Nicholas's words or tone deter him but said with equal firmness, "Yes, this is true. When I am up there, I can see farther and—"

"Stop!" Nicholas interrupted him harshly. "Guards are not allowed to leave their posts under any circumstances! That's *not* the way we do it here. Ever! You know that! What could you possibly have been thinking? Your lack of discipline is exceptionally disappointing and, under the circumstances, inexcusable. We need complete confidence that guards are doing their jobs. I will be forced to bring your case in front of the Council to find another use for you. You will not be able to serve as guard anymore."

Ayo could not believe what he was hearing. "Nicholas, I have found a way to make guarding so much better . . ."

"Ayo, your good intentions don't matter. I have no time to discuss the matter further. I am truly sorry." Nicholas turned around and left the scene.

Ayo was dumbfounded. He stumbled, then collapsed near a bush. He didn't know if he was about to scream— or cry.

When Nadia heard how her hero older brother had

behaved, she too was dumbfounded. She tried to find Nicholas but was told he was in a meeting. So she spent time with Ayo.

The two frustrated, confused, dispirited Meerkats talked much, until Ayo became quiet, staring off at nothing in particular. Then he said, "Nadia, I cannot live this way. I am unable to help. I am failing. It is insane. I am leaving the clan. I will find another clan where maybe I can be of some use."

Nadia looked horrified.

"I won't be the first to go," Ayo told her. "The best burrow-maker and two others left yesterday." Nadia had heard a rumor that Zuberi, the burrows guy, and maybe a few of his very capable friends had left.

Next to Nicholas, Ayo was dearest to Nadia's heart. She could not imagine how her friend, who knew of very little except guarding, could survive out in the desert all by himself. "In that case," she blurted out impulsively, "I am going with you!"

An idea had been developing in her mind for days. Other Meerkat clans, she thought, must be facing similar problems. What were they doing? Surely at least one clan had discovered a better way, yes? Someone must find out and then bring that knowledge back to her friends and family.

She explained her unusual idea to Ayo. They discussed it. And they agreed: Why, indeed, shouldn't the "someone" be the two of them?

Nadia looked again for Nicolas, this time to let him know that she and Ayo had decided to leave and go look for a solution that was better than the way the clan was trying to deal with all the new challenges. As always, he was in a hurry and just rushed by her as she spoke.

"*Nicholas, are you listening?*" she shouted louder than she wanted. "I am leaving."

He stopped examining his long list of things he needed to do and looked up at his sister. "What are you talking about? You can't be serious. What's wrong, Nadia?"

"Everything is wrong!" she said. "The clan is falling apart and all the Council is doing is telling and yelling, and I am so tired of it."

Then the frustration of the past few weeks poured out of her. "I am tired of watching how you exhaust yourself. I am tired of seeing some of us seeming to care only for ourselves. I am tired of listening to endless talk about who is to blame. I am tired of no one listening to those who have ideas to make things better that go beyond what you all seem to see as the best and only way. I am sick of watching those who want to help get pushed back into their place and told to shut up and wait for orders. And the Council, including you, act as if you don't even see all this."

She explained her idea of looking for clans that were doing a better job of dealing with these new threats and then bringing that information back. Nicholas stared at her as if she were speaking in an unknown language.

"Things will get better again," he said, only half convinced. "My guards have worked successfully on a number of schemes in just the past few days. And you yourself have come to realize we have great strengths that have helped us prosper for years."

Nadia nodded wearily, and said no more—realizing she had nothing else to say.

"It is too dangerous to rove around!" Nicholas said. "You know that."

"Yes, I know, Nicholas," she said, "and it scares me quite a bit. But there is no hope here. And without hope, life is unacceptable. Maybe Ayo and I won't find any clan doing better than we are—but I can't believe that. And we have to try."

Meerkats have a unique ability to literally close their ears, an invention of nature to protect their heads from sand when they are digging burrows. He was not digging burrows, but Nadia could see that her brother's ears were tightly closed.

She hugged Nicholas for a long moment, then pushed him away, turned quickly, and ran so he wouldn't see her tears. She spent the last hours in the afternoon arranging for another Older Sister to take responsibility for her pups, and thinking.

It did not make sense. So soon after she had come to

believe what her brother and the clan did so well, that this Kat-management was truly amazing, it was now totally failing to deal with their problems.

These boxes and plans and rules could not cope with . . . with what? The vulture? But she knew that wasn't quite right. It was something broader. It was about new challenges

for which they did not have established solutions and policies, challenges coming at them so quickly. With all the change, the Kat-management just started more telling and yelling from the bosses, yet that didn't help. It rejected creative ideas like Ayo's because that was not the way they did things, a way that had worked so well for so long. And that didn't help.

At sunset, Ayo and Nadia left.

Chapter 3

The Journey

Nadia and Ayo decided to walk as fast as possible during the night and sleep in abandoned burrows during the day. That way they would move a little more slowly but be much safer.

It took them two nights to find another clan. Arriving just before dawn, they sat and waited for the Meerkats to awaken. When the Kats came out their burrows, the two travelers estimated that there might be sixty or eighty of them.

"Strange," Nadia told Ayo, "no one even seems to take notice of us."

"Lousy guards," he replied.

They sat observing the clan. It was not a pretty sight.

They could see immediately that the level of anxiety here made anything back in their family look relatively calm. Although most of the Meerkats were running around, it was not at all obvious that much was being accomplished. Those who seemed to be in charge were doing the telling and yelling like those at home, but it was mostly yelling. And it did not appear that even routine tasks—feeding pups, fixing a collapsed burrow—were being done well.

When Nadia tried to speak with clan members, she almost always heard, "Sorry, I am in a rush, I have no time. I must . . ." And off the Meerkats went. When she was finally able to stop one harried fellow, she learned that this clan had to cope with many of the same challenges as her clan back home. But as much as she could tell, all the things Nicholas routinely did each day as Head of Guards, even under the suddenly difficult conditions, were nearly foreign to this group. And as for revolutionary ideas to deal with the terrible new circumstances, she heard no evidence of any.

It was not difficult to figure out who were the Alphas of the clan. A crowd of some eight to ten Meerkats sort of slithered behind them wherever they would go. As for the rest of the clan, pretty much all the others seemed to try to avoid the bosses and slitherers by moving in other directions when they showed up nearby.

Nadia and Ayo talked much that evening. They could not help but feel this clan was doomed. What a horrible thought.

There are lessons here, Nadia thought, but she needed some time to think more clearly about what they were. It was clear, though, that staying around the doomed, and unable to help them at all, made no sense.

The two travelers left after staying only a day.

They quickly encountered other clans. But with the drought, most were not welcoming any new members, and a few even chased them away. Others were like the doomed or appeared to be just a smaller version of their home clan.

Walking in the cold nights, eating less than their regular portions of food, and trying to sleep during the day quickly started to take a toll on them. But every time one of them wondered aloud if they should keep looking, the other found words or gestures of encouragement. So they kept moving.

Occasionally they met other rovers. But most of them were . . . a bit strange. So they were initially skeptical when they ran into Matt.

Matt was taller than most Meerkats and a bit older than either Nadia or Ayo. From what they could tell, he had been wandering around for quite a while.

After some rover-meets-rover small talk, Nadia asked him how he came to be walking in the Kalahari alone.

Matt's story was a tragic one, of a clan that found no solutions to the new threats and eventually disintegrated. Families fell apart. Guarding became erratic. In the end, only the burrows were meticulously kept, even expanded, with only half the burrow force to do the work. And Matt was a burrows Beta.

Ayo immediately liked the new Meerkat, because he obviously had high standards and was very serious about his work. Nadia immediately thought of her brother, whom she was already missing dearly, and who she guessed shared much in common with Matt.

"Join us," she impulsively said to Matt. Ayo paused, obviously thinking, then nodded. Matt was surprised but pleased, and quickly agreed.

The three rested briefly. Matt told his new companions, "I have heard about a clan that is newly formed, easily accepts new members, has enough food, and is not being killed off by the vulture or all the new snakes."

That certainly drew Nadia's and Ayo's attention.

"I haven't been able to find them despite looking for three days now." Matt drew in the dirt a meticulously detailed map that he had created of the plain from his excursions. "They are said to be around here," he told them, pointing to one spot.

Ayo grabbed Matt and pulled him to a large tree nearby. He told Matt to follow him up and in less than a minute they were at the very top.

"Now, where would you put a clan in this plain?" Ayo asked.

"Wow," Matt said, much as Nadia had when she first saw the view from the top of a tree. It took a moment to take in this spectacular new perspective and make sense of everything he saw. Then after a short pause he pointed to a place some five kilometers away. "There!" he said.

They traveled again at night. The next morning, Nadia, Ayo, and Matt found a small clan. And it required only a few minutes to see that it was different.

A Very Different Way

There were only a dozen Kats in the clan and they all sat in a circle together. They appeared to be beginning a meeting just as Nadia, Ayo, and Matt arrived. Those who saw the new trio smiled, or at least didn't look hostile. The Kat leading the group, whom they later learned was Lena, the founder of the clan, asked the rovers to sit near the group and wait until the session was over. Then she opened the meeting with:

"We know the rain is late this year, later than ever. We have been clever so far in not allowing this to be much of a problem." She smiled at the others. "We don't understand why this is happening and we cannot make it rain."

Two Meerkats softly chuckled.

"But," she continued, "what we can do is be prepared if rain will not come tomorrow or the next day or the week after next. Yes?"

The others nodded tentatively.

"Not that we would ever wish for this problem—but a clever solution can make us an even stronger and better clan. So we have an opportunity here."

Lena smiled yet again and most of the group nodded yet again. Nadia was mesmerized.

Lena continued. "Does anyone want to help us talk about how we can better deal with this . . . opportunity?"

A shy hand went up first, almost unnoticed, but Lena immediately said, "Yes. Tamu. Let's give Tamu a round of applause."

And they actually did. Those who knew that Lena had

encouraged Tamu to volunteer smiled and clapped their hands the loudest.

"Let's first collect some ideas," Tamu said tentatively and quietly. "Please do not comment on any yet. First, just collect them."

The Meerkats shouted out their thoughts. Tamu wrote each idea in the soil in different places within the meeting court. When one suggestion came out, but before Tamu could write it in the dirt, another Kat shouted a thought for how to improve it. The idea's originator paused for only a second, then smiled and nodded vigorously.

When Tamu had seven suggestions, and no further ideas were raised, he asked the others to vote with their feet by going to the idea they liked most. All except two of the Kats went to one of three suggestions. Tamu suggested they focus on those three, and the rest of the group readily agreed. He asked his fellow clan-colleagues to explain what they liked about their favorite proposal among the three. He then asked the others what potential problems they saw with each of those ideas.

The discussion that followed shaped two of the three

ideas in new ways that strengthened what the Kats liked and reduced what they didn't. Nadia watched it all with eyes that seemed to her twice the size as normal. She had never seen anything remotely like this before.

"Can we do all three of these?" Tamu asked in the end.

"No!" was the clear answer from almost all in the group.

"Are you willing to support the idea that gets the most votes?"

"Yes!" was the loud response from the group.

So they voted one more time with their feet and produced a rather unambiguous winner. It was the "share the food" idea.

The concept was simple, but difficult to implement because of all sorts of barriers. "Share the food" meant you no longer ate what you found. You would, somehow, collect any surplus beyond what a Kat absolutely needed and make sure it was available to those in need. Simple concept, yet a pretty radical idea in the Meerkat world.

"What about the runner-up idea?" Tamu asked.

Someone suggested that they keep it in mind and, if the share-the-food solution wasn't practical, come back to it. The group seemed to agree. Then they looked at Lena, who smiled and nodded.

"We will need some volunteers," she told them, "to lead the way in helping us figure out how exactly to do share-the-food and then to actually make it happen. Who wants to help?"

Five hands went up. "Very good," said Lena. "Let's thank Tamu for a very productive discussion." All did, and the meeting ended.

As the clan dispersed, the Meerkat who had started and ended the session came over to the three newcomers. "Hi, I am Lena. And who are you?"

They introduced themselves and briefly told her their stories. Lena listened without interrupting. When they finished, she told them she would be delighted if they joined the clan. In reply, they said that they would be honored to do so.

"And what about the vulture?" Ayo asked. "Has it been here as well?"

"Oh yes," Lena said. "It didn't do any damage, although it certainly tried. All of us are what clans typically call 'guards.' So when one of our group saw it, he yelled as loud as possible, we all heard him, we jumped into burrows, and that was that. After the first attack, Satu led a group that helped develop an idea which is making us even safer. You should talk to him and let him explain it to you. He would enjoy that. We haven't seen the vulture for a while. There must be other places where it can get its meals with less effort and frustration."

Another Meerkat called Lena's name and she excused herself to attend to a group member who was apparently ill.

Nadia had so many questions, she was not sure where to begin. But first, she and Ayo and Matt found some food and got some rest. When she awoke, she immediately asked how to get an appointment with Lena and only received stares back. "Just go talk to her," everyone said. Which Nadia did.

Share-the-Food and Other Unusual Ideas

Nadia learned that the clan was only a few months old. It had been founded by Lena and seven others who had broken away from a larger clan because they hated the way it was run. Now they did it their way.

To better understand how they operated, Lena encouraged Nadia to attend the first meeting that afternoon of the share-the-food team of volunteers. And she did.

Tamu arrived a bit late and the group was already sitting comfortably under the shade of the large tree that marked their meeting court. "Sorry for being late," Tamu said.

"Not a problem," said one of the others. "We have just talked about who we would like to lead the team." Tamu found all eyes looking at him. They were friendly, encouraging looks. Still, it all made him a bit uncomfortable.

"You mean . . . ?" he asked.

"Yes, Tamu," one Kat said. "We would like you to lead the team. Would you accept?"

Many thoughts and anxious feelings rushed through his mind. But it was a happy moment. He had played no role of any importance in his old clan. And he had roved around, lonely and scared, searching for a new home after his family clan had fallen apart. "I accept," he heard himself say. A few of the others clapped their paws.

For the rest of the meeting they talked about what success in sharing food would look like, how to help the clan see the virtue of that vision, and what could be done to motivate others to make it a reality as quickly as possible.

"Can't we just give out the order to share food?" an impatient new member of the clan suggested. But another said, "In our clan, no one has the right to order others to do anything. That's not the way we do it here."

The newcomer blinked twice. He was not totally surprised in light of what he had experienced since joining the group. Still, it was a pretty radical way of doing things.

The discussion of how you might make a share-the-food idea actually work went back and forth until someone finally suggested, "We have fifteen Meerkats in our clan if you count our latest newcomers, and we have five in our team. What if the five of us just start sharing our catch?"

In the absence of any better idea, they concluded it was worth trying, and so they did.

The next day they sat in a half circle and all put their catch on a plate that one team member had made from a hollow piece of wood decorated with leaves. It didn't take long until the first few curious fellows arrived at this rather strange scene, some of them quite hungry. The next day, eight Meerkats met at the same place sharing their food; the day after that, ten. Nadia thought that those who picked food from the plate one day tried harder the next to catch and bring food to the clan lunch. No one tried to count or keep records, or seemed at all inclined to try, but it did appear that the Kats found more food, certainly not less, than before the sharing routine began.

The five-Kat share-the-food team celebrated their success when they next met. Lena joined them, congratulating all on the vision and creative achievement. And in many conversations she had during the coming days, she would casually but frequently mention how proud she was of those coming to the community lunch and sharing their catch.

Nadia loved all she was seeing. It took only a few days until the two puppies in the clan adopted her as a sort of "older sister," wanting to spend as much time as possible with her. She was happy to do so, but checked first to see who was officially in charge of the pups. She learned that no one was because there were no "jobs" in the sense that she knew them. No head or guards. No Family Chiefs. There was one other Meerkat who volunteered to help the puppies grow up and to watch over them, and he welcomed Nadia to work with him. The two of them began to meet occasionally to share what worked well, what did not, and how to become better at helping the pups.

Meanwhile, Ayo had been scanning the area for the best guarding posts. He quickly saw a half dozen ways in which they could improve guarding. Some of the more junior Meerkats were fascinated watching and listening to him and asked for lessons in guarding skills. He happily accepted.

Matt inspected the burrows and found that they were not in particularly good shape. When he spoke with Lena about it, she beamed and asked him to find a few volunteers to do what he could. Which he did.

Tamu, for his part, literally stumbled over a potentially big idea. It came to him in the form of a gigantic (for him) elephant dropping.

After cleaning his paw, he noticed in the pile hundreds if not thousands of small white bugs. He examined a few, cleaned them in the sand, and tasted them, initially with a most serious frown on his face. But his face lit up quickly because he discovered they were quite delicious and juicy. Then a flash went through his head. What if they collected elephant droppings and created a kind of little-creatures-for-food farm to complement their catch? Could this be an important solution to their food problem?

Tamu explained his concept to the others. Few were enthusiastic about eating tiny creatures that came from a piece of you-know-what, much less about helping to form balls from those droppings, to roll them to a chosen site, and to create the farm. The unenthusiastic were told, "Fine, you don't have to."

And most did not. But it still didn't take long until he had a few volunteers wanting to try to move the idea into action. He informed Lena, and in her usual upbeat manner she encouraged them to go, try, learn, and improve.

There was still a lot to discover and learn about this new farming endeavor, and the Meerkats who wanted to help made much happen very quickly. Their first "harvest" was added to the shared-food plate. Although cautious at first, more and more Meerkats came to try and like the new offering.

Nadia watched all this very closely. She was amazed

at so much of it: The speed with which new important ideas were created, supported, and made to happen. The enthusiasm, the degree of cooperation, and the energy level. In her mind, she constantly compared it to what she had known all her life. This was so radically different, yet it was working so well. Her curious nature kept thinking: *But why? Why?*

She went to see Lena.

Circles Versus Squares, Want to Versus Have To

"Lena, what holds this clan together? What allows it to be so . . ." Nadia was searching for words like "energized" and "creative."

After some thought, Lena drew some circles into the sand that would look to humans like a solar system, with a sun, planets, and a few moons.

"In the center," Lena said, "we have the group that comes together weekly to talk about what we stand for, who we want to be, and the central issues facing the clan. I guess it is the spirit of brotherhood and sisterhood that brings and holds us together. You cannot fail here, unless you fail to try."

"Can everyone come to those weekly meetings?" asked Nadia

"When there was only a dozen of us, yes. Now that more and more rovers like you are joining us, I suppose one day we will encourage many to help in other ways. It seems as if not everyone enjoys the hard work of thinking about big questions, much less listening to the opinions of others—all the others."

Nadia pointed to the planets and moons in the solar system diagram. "And what are these other circles all about?"

Lena nodded. "Today, one is about our bug farm, started by Tamu, one is about caring for pups, which you initiated, and one organizes the food-sharing activity, now led by Alonda."

She drew a few circles around Alonda's circle. "And each of these groups has a number of activities going on. I can't keep track of them all. I suppose I don't even try. These activities are led by . . . well, it could be anyone. I am often surprised who turns out to have the passion and vision.

"As you have seen, each group selects its leader. And you can join any group you want."

Nadia looked at the image and thought about Lena's words. It was hard to understand in light of all she had experienced in her life, yet it made a lot of sense.

Just before dusk, two roaming Meerkats from a clan that had been destroyed by a vulture and starvation arrived. They were as astonished as Nadia about what they saw and heard, and one immediately went searching for other remnants of his group.

And thus the Lena clan continued to grow, and quickly. With safety and food and good cheer, a few big litters came quickly. The word somehow spread and other roaming Meerkats found them. The group of twelve when Nadia arrived grew to twenty, and then to thirty with astonishing speed.

Nadia, Ayo, and Matt quickly became important members of the group. But unlike Matt and Ayo, who had found what they had been looking for, Nadia knew she needed to go home very soon and share what she was learning:

About the power of leadership from anywhere, about passion, vision, volunteering, and creativity—without ANY boxes, lines, procedures, and Alphas/Betas. About how it was possible to deal with totally new and unknown challenges with astonishing speed.

Lena's clan continued to grow quickly. It hit fifty . . . which was where the problems began.

Chapter 4

With Size Comes...

Matt began to create a detailed map of the burrows. It showed where some were not being maintained well and areas that were missing sufficient underground tunnels to accommodate the growing clan. He found a few fellow clan members who were excited about the intellectual challenge of mapping, calculating, and designing burrows. But when he asked for volunteers to help dig and clean the tunnels, meeting each morning at eight o'clock sharp, the response was less than enthusiastic.

"Each morning at eight o'clock sharp? Eight o'clock? I'd like to help, but . . ."

"We would dig and clean according to a detailed plan? Well, Matt, this is not really my thing."

With Ayo's help, Matt also mapped out as best he could how guarding was being done. The Meerkats were highly dedicated to protecting each other, but their efforts were erratic. And, as with burrows, although some were more than willing to help Ayo plan how guarding should be done, the number willing to follow a schedule, guard at night ("boring!"), and follow orders was . . . not a lot.

Ayo and Matt went to Lena.

"We are concerned with safety, Lena. We are now large enough to attract attention. To protect the clan, we would need at least three, better yet four, trained guards on duty all day and night. And they have to be in the right places, so there must be a firm schedule to obey. The idea that 'everybody watches for everybody' isn't sensible anymore."

Lena listened as Matt also described the problem with Kats not showing up on time to dig and maintain burrows. Then she said, "Look around, Ayo. Matt. Life is good for us. Even with a drought, we just had three new litters. Almost daily we have new Meerkats joining. You may be worrying too much."

But although she said nothing, even Lena was beginning to notice with increasing concern necessary work not being done, or done reliably every day. On guarding and burrows, she wished Matt and Ayo would provide more leadership to sort out whatever issues there were. But she did not want to criticize them and deflate their commitment and enthusiasm. So she gave them one of her you-can-do-it speeches.

At the next weekly meeting, Lena spoke about the ideals of the clan. She was inspiring, as always, but she was mostly talking to those who did not need the talk. And because the meetings were a "want to" event, the people who most needed to be there to hear her were absent.

Over the coming days, tensions within the clan between old-timers and new arrivals, the Matt-like Meerkats and the not-Matt-like Meerkats, and the givers and takers grew further.

Everything that required some form of coordinated effort among dozens of Meerkats was either not done reliably or was debated endlessly in groups that were increasingly frustrated with each other for their inability to get things done. Even those who wanted to help were often in the dark on what was expected or were playfully pouring a great deal of time and creativity into tasks that just needed to be done in a certain way that some of the others already knew.

Nadia, Ayo, Matt, and Tamu went to Lena and told

her that they needed to talk. When Lena asked what was bothering them—and something obviously was bothering them—she heard:

- After the initial excitement around bug farming, Tamu found it harder and harder to get enough volunteers to do the routine work, which realistically was not all pleasant. He spent so many hours himself doing the farming that he was starting to feel exhausted.
- Nadia reported that some of the clan who had volunteered to help with new litters were just not suitable for the role. But who should tell them? Who had the right to tell them?
- Matt explained to Lena and the others that despite his best efforts, the burrows were in chronically poor condition. No one was eager or, apparently, had the skill to build and maintain these spots.
- And Ayo just told her, "You know what I think about safety and guarding."

There were still more complaints. Lena listened, sighed, and then said, "When I founded this clan with some friends, we envisioned in each of us both a servant and a leader. In all of us is a deep desire to show up every day and be the best we can be." And after a dramatic pause: "Do you believe this to be worthy and true?" The others nodded slowly in a way that seemed to say, "Well, yes, but . . ." Lena then spoke about how she was sure the clan and its strong spirit would be able to overcome the issues that appeared to be a natural part of growing.

Nadia, Ayo, Matt, and Tamu left the meeting somewhat more upbeat, wondering how Lena had once again been able to seemingly shrink problems and boost confidence.

Finally the Rain Comes

Over the coming days Matt spoke often with Nadia. The more he studied the burrows, the more he became additionally alarmed. So that night he didn't sleep well again, staying awake thinking of how to tackle the problem. When he first heard *plop, plop,* he didn't immediately know what it was. Then the noise began to grow louder until it was roaring.

The rain had arrived.

Matt ran out and saw how the dry soil quickly soaked up the pouring water. But it did not take long before there were a few inches of liquid covering a surface that could not absorb it fast enough. Matt didn't panic easily, but his mind required little time to draw the obvious, frightening conclusion: Very soon the water would pour into the burrows. Given the weak condition of some of the tunnels, they would certainly collapse.

"Rain! Wake up! Get out!" he shouted, racing back into his burrow.

Some Meerkats reacted quickly and came running out,

dragging puppies with them who had no idea what was going on because they had never seen rain in their young lives. Matt ran to another burrow to give the alarm. But it was already too late. The tunnel had collapsed, filling fast with water and trapping the sleeping Meerkats.

"Help! Help!" Matt shouted. A few others quickly gathered around him and together they began to dig a new channel into a burrow where the main entrance was already overflowing with water. Matt knew the best and fastest path from his mapping, but it wasn't clear whether the Meerkats were still in the main cave or had retreated into an intact side channel. When they finally heard panicked shrieks coming from within the burrow they knew they were on the right track. Shortly thereafter the scared-to-death fellows were hugging their exhausted saviors.

Matt pushed a still terrified but joyous Kat away from him as he heard more screams to his left and to his right. "Come on!" he yelled to all around him. "There is much work to do still!"

Risking his own life, and with the help of a few others, Matt repeated what he had just done. Six more were saved. But the burrows were a mess. The lack of systematic maintenance had taken its toll.

Seven Meerkats died that night. Those who survived were stunned.

The next day, Kats sat around by themselves or talked quietly in small groups. There was much sadness and mourning. But more so, the growing tension of the past few weeks finally found its escape valve. The search for whom to blame began in earnest.

Some of the early clan members glorified the good old days when they were still small and everyone truly cared for each other. They blamed the current problems on those who had recently joined the group. "We are just not the same anymore and it is their fault! They need to go!"

The "givers" blamed all those who talked smart but never reliably showed up each day for work. "I am tired of covering for someone else. This want-to idea is nonsense and out of touch with reality!"

Others were debating about the need for someone to take charge of the chaotic situation and to bring order out of the chaos by ruling with a firm hand.

And Lena was in the middle of it. Although she tried not to let it show, she was shaken that her vision of how a clan should operate was falling apart and wondering what had happened.

Nadia could not believe that, once again, her world was crumbling before her eyes. Her legs more or less gave out and she sat. Time went by. An hour? Two? Many thoughts went through her mind, most of them confused or sad or discouraged.

What she had so quickly learned to love, all the energy and passion and vision and leadership, even from junior members of the group, what she was coming to believe was clearly a better way to run a clan was . . . totally failing.

But why? She pictured the small number of Kats when she arrived and the much larger group now. She thought of the discipline and structure and rules that her brother, and Matt, believed were so important and were missing here— to their detriment? But that Kat-management had failed back in her home clan!

And then the proverbial light bulb went on.

Chapter 5

The following morning was bright and clear. So was Nadia's mind.

"Lena, we have to talk," she said when she located the clan's founder under the community tree.

An exasperated Lena asked Nadia to sit down. Nadia looked at her and said, "You are an amazing leader, Lena, you truly are."

Lena's eyes drifted down until she was staring at her hands. "That is kind of you, Nadia, but under the circumstances . . ."

Nadia gently touched her new friend until she looked up again. "You're unquestionably the most inspiring and supportive person I have ever met in my life."

The two just stared at each other, then Lena said softly, "Thank you, Nadia. Your opinion means a lot to me."

"When we joined the clan," Nadia continued, "I was immediately taken by the spirit of this place, which *you* established. It brought out the best in many of us and has made marvelous things like the bug farm and the sharing of food happen, and happen so quickly."

"It wasn't me, Nadia," Lena interrupted gently. "It was the ideals and our vision. It was a group that came together and passionately believed in that. It was all the fearless energy and creativity this helped produce, aided, I suppose, by some encouragement by me here and there to keep people optimistic despite obstacles and setbacks."

Lena had stayed awake most of the night thinking about *why* it had all gone wrong. But Nadia had a better question.

"*When* did this start to go"—Nadia slowed, then plunged ahead—"to fall apart?"

If Lena was offended or feeling defensive, she did not show it. "In hindsight," she said, "maybe when we grew to a clan of thirty or so. Maybe you just can't have a great clan with more than twenty-five Meerkats."

Nadia shook her head. This was all making sense.

"In my home clan, there were one hundred and fifty of us! And we never had a burrow collapse, or unattended guarding posts, or Kats who were not suitable for the task in charge of pups. Everyone had a role and a contribution to make to earn the right to be a part of the clan. And they did their jobs well!"

Nadia drew Lena's circle diagram into the sand. "These circles and the principles behind them can't achieve this. They can motivate us to act and innovate with great energy, and sometimes with astonishing speed. But I do not see how they can ensure that a large clan gets the routine daily work done reliably."

Nadia then drew lines and boxes next to Lena's circles diagram and heard herself repeating what Nicholas had told her not so long ago about managing.

Lena listened. Her eyes looked at the new diagram with an intensity. She nodded gently as Nadia spoke. You could tell by her expression that she was absorbing these new ideas, or at least trying greatly to do so.

Much of what Nadia said sounded to Lena like the clan she had grown up in and left. But Nadia's method was more logical and sophisticated and less arbitrary. It was not filled with obviously silly rules and rulers who should not be in their positions.

When Nadia finished her Nicholas-speech, Lena pointed to the two drawings in the dirt and, anticipating where Nadia was going next, said, "But they are so different. How could they ever go together?"

Nadia thought for a moment. "Lena, are you creative and open to new, even crazy-sounding ideas?"

"I hope so," Lena answered.

Nadia's eyes grew larger. "Hope! Of course you are! Yet aren't you disciplined and planful enough to get things done?"

Lena paused, then said, "Not nearly as much as some Meerkats I have known. But yes."

It didn't take Lena long to see the lesson in her own

answers. "You mean if a single Meerkat can be both creative and disciplined, at least to some degree, then why couldn't a clan?" she said, pointing to the two drawings.

Nadia nodded.

"But if I had to do those things that you call 'management' all day long, I think I would collapse. Or go crazy," Lena said.

"Why should you have to?" asked Nadia with a smile. "Have you ever seen a Meerkat with the gifts to do everything extremely well? I haven't. Yet we sometimes achieve a lot—by working together."

Lena's mind was racing. She had so many unanswered questions on how to make two very different types of clans work together to get the benefits of both while avoiding the limitations of either. But never in her life had she needed all the answers, just a promising direction.

"Would you help me make this work?"

Nadia looked torn. She said, "I can't, Lena. I'm not your perfect companion in this. And I have to go back now to my home clan and tell them about what I have discovered. I hope you know how much I care about you and the others here. But I have to at least try to help the Kats who raised me, and I miss my older brother deeply. Besides, you have exactly what you need here already."

Nadia looked around—and quickly found what she was searching for. Lena followed Nadia's eyes and saw it too.

"Matt?" Lena asked.

"Sure. He is a fantastic manager and smart enough to see this idea." Nadia pointed to the two diagrams. "He respects you greatly," she added, "and you seem to respect him."

Neither Meerkat said anything for a few moments. Then Lena asked, "But I have never seen a clan work like this before. Have you?"

Nadia smiled. "And how many times had you seen a bug farm before?"

Neither said anything, then Lena smiled too. "When would you leave?" she asked.

"Tonight," Nadia replied.

Lena sighed, but quickly offered one of her warmest smiles. "I wish you all the best. And thank you for everything. Please come back anytime you want. You will always be welcome."

They hugged each other for what seemed like a long time. Then Nadia walked away.

The Big Opportunity

"I must go with you," Ayo said.

"But you have made a difference here," Nadia responded. "And I think you can help Lena and Matt. You have a great future in front of you—"

He interrupted her. "I would have a miserable future in front of me if something should happen to you on your way home. And if you haven't noticed, I find it rather impossible to be happy anywhere without you around!" an upset Ayo said, louder than he intended.

Nadia paused, looking at Ayo with some surprise and then a big smile. "Okay . . ."

"So what do we do next?" he asked.

She thought. "We walk by night again. We begin by meeting at the community tree as soon as it is dark."

He nodded in agreement.

Nadia continued. "Now I need to go and say farewell to my friends and invite anyone who would like to come with us. You should do the same."

He did. And at shortly past sunset, after some tearful good-byes, the two left with a handful of others who wished, for various reasons, to join them.

They went east, quickly retracing the path that Nadia and Ayo had taken before. They passed the spot where the doomed clan had been. No one was there. Not one Meerkat. The sight was depressing.

"Let's move faster," she said, and the small team did just that.

The following dawn they saw a group of rovers approaching. When they came closer, Nadia saw that they weren't real rovers. It was Nicholas with a few of his guards!

Brother and sister ran toward each other. When they met, the siblings hugged each other tightly. It was a very emotional reunion—great warmth, deep relief that each was safe. But in less than a minute, Nicholas stood back and his anger poured out.

"Why did you go? Where have you been? I have been worried to death!" He noticed the group of Meerkats with Nadia and Ayo. "And who are they?"

Nadia said, "I will explain everything. But first tell me what has happened back home."

So he did. The vulture attacks and the drought were bad enough. But then a sandstorm had locked the already weakened clan in the burrows for two days. They had no procedure for handling a two-day sandstorm while trying to deal with other unprecedented problems. The new hazards along with the clan's inability to deal with the problems had sent them further down a spiral of hunger, anger, and anxiety, which first stopped the clan's growth and then led it to actually shrink in size.

"We have had some successes. It's not all failure. We have learned some things about how to deal with the vulture," said Nicholas. "Slowly life is improving now." The word "slowly" sounded anguished, mad, and filled with frustration.

Nicholas turned to Ayo. "A few weeks ago I heard from one of my guards about your top-of-tree method. I have managed to get it adopted much of the time, but not all." Nicholas was embarrassed that some guards, for whatever reasons, were not following his orders to consistently work in this new way. "Your idea has made a difference, Ayo."

Ayo smiled broadly. Although he did not show it, he was nearly ecstatic that his innovation had finally been helping the clan.

The drought was mostly over, but the experience of failure had left one of the Alphas (Moro), Nicholas, and two Family Chiefs deeply concerned. What had they been missing? And even more worrisome, some of the clan seemed to be acting as if all was well enough now that there was no extreme crisis, as if the need to reflect on their experiences was not important.

"I think we have a solution," Nadia told her brother.

His eyes went wide. "Really?"

"Really."

"Tell me more."

"Later," Nadia said. "I don't know about the rest of you, but after walking the whole night, I am hungry and I need a nap, in that order."

Nadia looked around and saw clear agreement in the eyes of all the rovers. But before everyone could run in different directions to try to find crunchy insects, scorpions, and the like, she said, "We still have a long walk in front of us and we all need to be as strong as possible. We can only go as fast as the slowest. In the clan we have just come from we learned to share food that we did not absolutely need for ourselves."

A look of incomprehension surfaced on the faces of Nicholas and his guards.

"My friends will bring their catch," Nadia said, "to share with those who were not so lucky. And if you want to, you can do the same."

For Nicholas and his guards, this was a radical idea. His guards looked to him for guidance and he gave a hard-to-detect nod. And so within an hour they were all back together more or less sharing their catch, talking, and even occasionally laughing.

After a nap, Nicholas crawled out of the burrow to find Nadia already sitting under a tree. "How are you?" he asked his favorite little sister.

"I am so very happy to be with you again. I have missed you so much." And after a pause: "I need to explain what I have learned to the Alphas, Betas, and . . .

well, to all the rest of the clan. And I am not at all sure how to do that."

"How about starting with me?" Nicholas said as he scooted next to her. His face always showed respect when he was with Nadia, but if you looked closely you would have seen some suspicion that his younger sibling could have found any magical solution to a very difficult situation. "If you can get past me, others will be that much less of a challenge."

So Nadia told Nicholas, "You are a great manager, the best I have ever seen."

He of course was flattered.

"We have others in the clan who are at least good managers. But . . ." Nadia paused. "When do you think the problems in our clan started?"

He considered the question. "I guess," Nicholas answered, "the moment we were faced with the vulture, more snakes, and the drought. It all came at us so quickly and so unexpectedly. Never have I seen anything quite like this."

Nadia touched Nicholas's arm and said, "Lena's clan—that's where I have been living—had to cope with more or less the same challenges and, for a while at least, they did so brilliantly. Creatively. Fast. It was amazing."

She sketched Nicholas's drawing in the sand. "Our boxes and lines, Betas and Alphas, rules and procedures, measures and percentages, can't do what they did. Or at least I don't see how. Our way of life is built to help a large clan . . . to run well. To get the daily work done the way it is supposed to be done, and all the time. I now see clearly that that does not just happen. You have to be smart and disciplined when you have a group of fifty or one hundred or two hundred. But, forgive me, brother, what we are good at is pretty bad at dealing with almost anything that is new and unexpected, especially when a lot comes at you quickly."

Nicholas was a bit hurt, but in light of his recent experiences he couldn't really argue with her.

Nadia began to draw Lena's circles and explained to Nicholas what she had learned about how that way of life worked. She talked much about leadership, and not just from an Alpha but from anyone. He listened, trying to take it all in—but it was difficult. He had never seen anything quite like it.

Then she drew lines connecting the two diagrams, turning the two pictures into one.

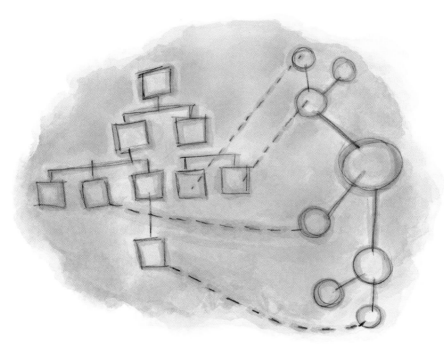

For the next few hours they talked and talked. Nicholas asked many questions: "But who would really be in charge? What if one of my guards is off working on one of those 'initiatives' and not guarding? We don't have enough Kats to fill all these jobs." Nadia tried to provide answers as best she could. But, honestly, she was occasionally just making a logical guess, because she had never really seen what she had drawn in the dirt.

When Nicholas kept staring off into the distance, his sister asked, "What are you thinking?"

He turned to her and wondered if he should share what was going through his head. Nadia said firmly, "This is no time to lie to your baby sister because you think she cannot deal with the truth."

Nicholas took a deep breath and said, "My fellow Betas, at least many of them, and at least one Alpha, will quite logically think this will produce chaos. They will think that expecting a young, inexperienced Kat to be in charge of an important project and to succeed is totally unrealistic. They would never allow these activities"—he pointed at the circles—"without clarity about who is the boss and defined measures showing whether the group is succeeding or not. Even if this were forced on them by the Alphas, the Betas, at least a few, would just naturally try to control it. Or kill it. They . . ."

He stopped when he saw his sister's face beginning to look discouraged. Maybe he had made a mistake in sharing these thoughts with her.

Nadia took a deep breath and closed her eyes. When she opened them, she said to her brother, "Is the clan thriving and growing? How well did it deal with the sandstorm crisis? Are you sleeping well at night knowing that your friends are safe? Is the clan living up to your hopes and dreams?" She paused, then continued. "If we need different results, are we going to get them by doing what we have always done, but just working harder?"

Nicholas silently stared at the ground for what seemed a long time. Then his chest expanded as he took a deep breath. He looked up at his sister and said only, "We have much important work to do."

That night they walked again, and the next morning they arrived at their old clan.

Trying to Explain

While Nadia had her hands full trying to calm down excited puppies who were hanging all over her, Nicholas sprang into action. He spoke briefly about what Nadia had told him to the three senior Meerkats who had been most supportive of his request to go look for his sister: one Alpha (Moro) and two Family Chiefs. All three struggled with what Nicholas was saying. But they did listen.

After questions, questions, and more questions, the others looked to Moro. The senior Meerkat gazed at the vast desert, which appeared to go on and on forever. "Most of the clan seems to think we are healing and that life will return to normal after a while." He moved his head from side to side slowly. "But I don't see it. There have been signs, maybe not dramatic signs, that our world is changing. And permanently. If that is so . . ."

The next day Moro spoke with his fellow big boss, Mara, about calling a meeting of all Betas and inviting Nadia. Mara looked at her fellow clan boss as if he had fallen on his head and was unwell. Listen to a young, inexperienced Kat who had abandoned the clan?! But Moro was softly yet firmly insistent. Without enthusiasm, but not wanting to start a fight, Mara finally agreed.

And so it came to be that Nadia talked to Moro, Mara, and all the Betas about the idea of two very different ways of working somehow melded together within one clan.

At a respectful distance, a few other adult Meerkats gathered to try to listen to this highly unusual conversation. A few became a dozen, then two dozen, and soon nearly half the adults and a few pups surrounded the bosses and Nadia. A single growl from both Alphas would have sent the crowd scurrying away. But though Mara grunted often, there was no joint growl.

Moro opened the meeting. "We all care for our fellow Meerkats too much to ever put them again at risk of sudden attacks and starvation, or possibly worse. We must remember, we are not alone in this world. There are many happy to take our place, eat our food, or, provided the opportunity, eat us. We cannot just settle, each of us doing our daily work or doing it a little better, and hope for the best."

Moro was talking to the Betas and Mara, but he was quite aware of the growing crowd. And he fully realized that all that he said was in fact being absorbed by the larger group.

"As many of you know, Nadia has been roving around and she has found what may be interesting lessons. I want you to listen carefully and help Mara and me to think this through."

Nicholas drew the diagram with the boxes and circles and Nadia began to tell the story of her journey. She talked about the clans she had encountered. She spoke of finally finding Lena's group and how they thrived and grew despite facing the threats of new predators and lack of rain. She spoke of how eventually their lack of the very skills her home clan had—that the Alphas and Betas had—created terrible problems after the thriving group grew beyond a certain point.

At the mention of "their crucial skills," a few of the Betas and Mara nodded knowingly.

Then Nadia talked about the circle of leaders, the energy and passion, the volunteering, the sense of vision, the willingness and ability to create and change, the bug farm, and the sharing of food. She spoke of how that clan thrived and grew—up to a point—when all others, including their own, struggled terribly after their world started to change so quickly.

The nodding from some Betas and Mara was replaced by looks of incomprehension and suspicion.

Moro listened intently and would occasionally even say "Yes"—quite unlike Mara. But even Moro wasn't the most patient of characters and had limited tolerance for just "what" might or should be done, so he began to push for a "how." How could they take these possible lessons and move forward in a way that was practical, that did not impose unacceptable risks, and that Kats could understand?

"Why don't we start with the bug farm?" Nadia blurted out. The clan still did not have all the food it needed. Nadia could see that this was both a daily problem for them and also an opportunity, maybe a big one, to help immediately and to demonstrate that something very different was possible and powerful.

Nicholas visibly nodded and sent encouraging looks to his sister.

She explained bug farming. Some of the Kats were confused, some appalled, but a few saw it for what it was, a potentially marvelous idea.

Two Betas asked questions, and then the debate began. When the conversation started to go in a bad direction, Nadia, almost channeling Lena, said, "We all love our fellow Meerkats too much to put them at risk of starvation again." She stood up in a way that almost looked like Lena. "We don't have to build a whole farm, or anything that is perfect. Just something that will help many of us see the true opportunities behind this idea."

Her face glowed with deep compassion and conviction. "We can figure out all this and make it happen if enough of us are willing to give it a chance." Pointing to the Alphas and Betas, she very respectfully added, "And the 'us' needs to start with you."

One Beta said, quite firmly, "But we are far too busy to spare Kats to build this farm thing."

Nadia nodded. "Fine. This is not about creating a farm

group that takes resources from the rest of you. Let's just see if we can find a few volunteers who would be willing to do their usual jobs plus work on the farm idea."

The Beta rolled his eyes, thinking, *But, realistically, why would anyone want to do this!?* What he then said out loud was, "Even if you are right, and your volunteers work long hours, they will at some point collapse of exhaustion and quit. So your project fails *and* they cannot do their regular job."

Without missing a beat Nadia replied, "What I saw at the Lena clan was that if Kats were tired or too busy elsewhere, they would drop out, not burn out. Eventually others would volunteer to take their place. It was not as if Lena or a Beta put pressure on those Kats and it was their extra job until the work was through. I think that made all the difference."

Another Beta immediately jumped into the conversation, firing questions: What about this and what about that, and that? Nicholas wanted to go over and slam each one of the vocal bosses on his or her head. But he knew that would not help.

And Nadia really did not need help. She knew she was right, and it showed. Her eyes flashed across the entire crowd and she told them, "I am not saying that we won't run into some problems. But I know that if enough of us believe in the opportunity to create a truly better, stronger, and safer clan, a clan that once again thrives and grows, we will start to make it happen despite—well, whatever."

The crowd stared at her. You could have heard a leaf falling from the community tree. This was not what a young Meerkat did in front of the bosses. And this was not the Nadia they knew from only a short time ago. She had changed.

Mara and a majority of the Betas were clearly unconvinced. But Moro stood to his full height and said firmly, "I think she is right about a possible opportunity here. We have a responsibility to the future of the clan, and to our pups. And if that requires adjustments to the way we work, even big adjustments, then it is our responsibility to take action."

He paused, looked at the entire crowd, and continued. "Is it easy to question a new idea? Especially if it is very different?" After stopping for a moment, he said, "Of course it is."

His face turned to look more directly at the Betas and Mara. "Shouldn't different circumstances require different ideas, possibly very different?" After a brief pause he finished the thought: "The only logical answer is yes."

Moro was far from channeling Lena, because their personalities were so different, yet there was the same strong and deep determination in his voice that was always in her speech.

And so with Moro taking a stand, Nicholas and one other Beta nodding vigorously, and the entire clan looking on, the other bosses eventually seemed willing to give something different a try—or at least not to block it.

With a surprisingly hopeful and yet partially suspicious smile, Moro said, "Who wants to help with the bug farm?"

The hands of Nicholas and the Family Chief who had been Nadia's teacher went up fastest. But so did a dozen others among Meerkats who had been creeping up closer to the front to hear the conversation.

Moro appeared a bit surprised, yet pleased. "Good." And in a most untraditional way he said, "If you need something, let me know." Then he closed the discussion.

Urgency, Leadership, Volunteering, and Wins

Nicholas went to see Nadia early the next morning. "What do you do next?" he asked.

She shook her head. "You're not putting this all on me, are you?"

"No," he told her, sounding a bit defensive. "I didn't mean it that way." He paused and then continued. "Okay, maybe I was. But I get your point now. What can I do to help?"

"Spread the word that you are excited about the opportunity to stop the hunger problems and build a safer clan. Point out that Moro seems to be backing this. Also, say that anyone who would like to volunteer for the bug farm should meet at noon under the community tree. I will do the same."

Nicholas nodded, and then Nadia asked, "I am of course thrilled at the way Moro is acting, but why do you think he seems to be supportive?"

Nicholas had been thinking about the same question.

"He cares deeply about the clan and cannot be at all happy about what has been happening. But I suppose you could say the same for Mara." Nicholas tilted his head, obviously thinking hard. "The only answer I have—and it is not much of an answer—is that Moro just instinctively seems to feel that something in your idea is right. I'm not sure. Anyway, let's get on with spreading the word."

And they did. At noon there were seventeen curious Meerkats showing some sense of urgency to turn this bug farm idea, or, in a few cases, anything truly new, into action. Nadia asked who wanted to lead, if only to facilitate a productive discussion. This, naturally, confused most of those present from her old clan who assumed the more senior of the two Betas at the session would take charge. But Nadia told them the story of Tamu, and Ayo helped the group work through the confusion, find a meeting facilitator, and get going.

They ran into what seemed like a new barrier every day. The burrows Beta pretty much ordered two of his Kats, who were supplying great energy to the farm team, to stop and just do their burrow's job. They did stop, and, pretty much just as Nadia had predicted, two other new volunteers jumped in to fill their roles. Kats would drop out—but there was no burnout, as some of the Betas had predicted.

Mara continued to give signals that she might never support the whole project. Nevertheless, Moro somehow behind the scenes kept stopping her from undermining the farm-building. But when a neighborhood clan invaded and hunted on the Moro/Mara territory more than once, she did successfully rally the Kats and diverted nearly all attention away from farming at a time when it very much needed attention. Yet as Nadia had predicted, a few volunteers refused to let the farming slow by working almost without sleep.

The energy from some of the volunteers was amazing. They did their regular jobs and worked any spare minute on the farm. Nadia and Nicholas were relentless. One other Beta, for whatever reason, started to act almost like Nicholas. And Moro, in his quiet, certainly not larger-than-life or charismatic way, made time in his busy schedule to visit the bug farmers, if only for a few minutes, every day. A smile here or a pat on the back there had an amazing effect. And the mere stories of Moro's visits spread throughout the clan with the speed of the strongest Kalahari wind.

When the first food started coming from the project, which happened with surprising speed, the volunteers invited the Alphas, the Betas, and everyone else to see for themselves what was happening with this unusual activity. It was one more unprecedented action, since regular Kats did not invite bosses to anything. But many of the bosses did come, including Moro, who arrived early.

The farm, even in its most elementary and early stages, left many of the Meerkats astonished and many others more inclined to want to hear from Nadia and Ayo about what else they had learned in their time away from the clan. And talk about the opportunity to do something significant for the clan only increased—especially when Moro and a number of the Betas began to speak on a regular basis about their big opportunity. Visible complacency—the actions of those who felt "we are okay now"—decreased almost daily. Anxieties and fears that were not leading to any useful outcomes also seemed to calm as a sense of urgency grew that they needed to do something new.

"What next?" Nicholas asked his sister.

Nadia thought. "I wish Lena were here."

Nicholas gave her a stern look. "But she isn't. So, I repeat, what next?"

"Maybe a circle of volunteer leaders, like Lena had, to help guide us. The very center of her diagram of circles. I think we now have enough interest and energy that it will be possible to create one."

And indeed it was possible. A core group of about a dozen started meeting regularly with Nadia and Nicholas. When Mara heard about it, she wanted to stop this unauthorized activity, but Moro prevailed. The core group began to choose where to put their energy. With a half dozen excited Kats, Ayo led the charge to find a way to make the new guarding idea work 100 percent across the entire clan. Again, it was easier said than done, but Ayo and his team were relentless. An older Meerkat who everyone assumed was no longer able to do much of anything volunteered to lead a sandstorm initiative. And, incredibly, with a newfound passion and thoughtfulness, he did. Credibility and momentum and urgency continued to grow as the members of the volunteer circle of leaders told their friends and family groups about the initiatives and their initial successes.

At the fifth meeting of the circle of leaders, a Meerkat named Pano showed up with a piece of fur stuffed with straw. It was shaped to have arms and legs and a head and eyes, and it was . . . well, cute.

Everyone stared at it. "Where did that come from?" one of the Kats asked.

"My sister made it," Pano told them. "I don't know how. But here is what she tells me that is really interesting. She says that if you give it to young Kats to hug when they are injured or ill, they seem to get better faster and with less need for others in our family group to spend time watching, feeding, and all the rest we normally do for the ill. She says she has seen this happen many times."

They all stared at the stuffed animal. Then someone

asked, "But if that is true, why don't we all know about it?"

Pano shrugged.

Someone said, "This is exciting. I want to talk to your sister and then try something on a broader basis if I can find a few others who would like to help. Okay?"

The circle of leaders discussed the strange idea. Not everyone immediately believed it would work, but one of the lessons this group had learned was that there was no reason for them all to agree. If someone found enough help to get an idea going, it was probably a promising one. Or at least worth trying.

And the Kat who asked to lead the healing effort had no problem finding a few others who wanted to move forward. Within a week the team had figured out how to make six more of the stuffed animals, none of them perfect or exactly alike, but all cuddly and cute. After two more weeks, they quietly tested the effect of these huggable creatures on four ill and four injured young Kats. In all cases, the pups embraced the new creations seemingly day and night. And in all but one case, they did seem to

get better faster and with less time-consuming care from adults! The team celebrated!

At first, a few of the Betas believed that they would be the only ones with the experience and knowledge to come up with intelligent new initiatives. Yet they found that even after years and years of "follow the rules and procedures," "just do what you are told," and "this is how we do things here," many creative ideas and energy poured out of some unpredictable places and unusual groupings of Meerkats who didn't work together as a part of their regular jobs. With time and, not surprisingly, some ups and downs, new groups learned to work together well and in a new way. They found ideas that individual Kats or the normal groupings could not seem to generate or see. They also found fascinating ways to overcome barriers, cope with normal resistance to change, and bring ideas to life.

Many of their new successes were seemingly small and relatively easy to do. But small adds up if it keeps coming and coming. And even though the speed was slower and the conflicts larger than Nadia had wanted, a new way of operating grew.

The circle of leaders met weekly to communicate, guide, inspire, and celebrate successes. The two most senior Kats in that group, Nicholas and one Family Chief, started to meet regularly with Moro, Mara, and the Betas to talk about the various initiatives that were being worked on. This made Mara and two Betas, who still worried that order and discipline would surely break down, a little more comfortable. And Moro seemed to grow with each meeting, not only in making sure these sessions were productive, but as a leader in general.

Moro and a few of the Betas also used what they were learning in the sessions outside the meetings. They began to pay closer attention to voluntary action, and to leadership from Kats not in official leadership positions. They occasionally would even go to a junior Meerkat and tell him or her how proud they were of some success, even a little success, that the junior Meerkat had helped make possible. When they saw the effect it had, they wondered, *Why haven't we always done this?*

Except when it was new and small, the clan had never seen so much excitement, energy, and leadership on various issues coming from so many Meerkats. They gave extra effort to better their lives and the life of the clan, no matter what new circumstances were thrown at them by weather or predators or whatever. And yet at the same time, the fears that discipline, intelligent procedures, and the like would inevitably break down or come into constant conflict with the new activities proved to be mostly overblown. If anything, with the removal of all the impossible stresses and strains placed on the bosses—the hierarchy, the procedures, and the rest of the traditional way of running the clan—they seemed to do a *better* job of making sure the guarding, burrowing, feeding, and managing of families proceeded well each and every day. And certainly some exhausted Betas and other Meerkats became less exhausted—and happier with life.

Dozens of Meerkats who certainly had never thought of themselves as leaders were in fact growing into leaders, writ big and small. For the most part, they loved this, and again for reasons that were often hard to explain. Their lives often seemed more interesting or exciting. And for more than a few among both young and old, their lives felt more purposeful and meaningful—even possibly Moro himself.

The farm continued to grow. Its success helped keep complacency at bay and created a stronger belief that pursuing more opportunities was needed. And because the farm already had been worked on in Lena's group, the volunteers needed surprisingly little time to find policies and procedures for running it well. As it became an increasingly essential part of feeding what was now a growing clan, the volunteers were asked to hand it over five months later to a newly appointed Beta, who was now officially in charge—to manage it with her own staff, plans, rules, measures, and procedures. The metrics showed that the farm was producing 25 percent of the clan's food supply with only seven Kats focused on this specialized task.

The work with the stuffed animals became a formally recognized healing initiative that brought together those who cared especially about the injured and ill. Over time, they discovered that caring for those hurt was a unique skill, backed by some "Kat-science" of sorts. The Alphas decided to create a new job, caregivers, and designate a Head Caregiver who worked inside one of the family groups but served the entire clan. When Nicholas told Nadia about this decision, she was thrilled.

"It will help the ill and injured so much. And it is more proof that the idea of a Lena clan and our old type of clan working together as one is not just an idealistic yet unrealistic hope." She was beaming.

Nicholas nodded. He looked at some point off in the distance, obviously thinking to himself.

"What?" Nadia asked.

"I would never have believed that the Alphas, much less the Betas, would have agreed to all this new activity."

"So why have they?" Nadia asked.

"I'm not entirely sure," was Nicholas's response. "Certainly evidence that this big idea is not, as you put it, 'idealistic nonsense'—that has helped a great deal. Your stories of your time away—really, they were educating us—that has helped. The sheer excitement . . . Passion has been like a good disease, spreading from one Kat to

another. I think we Betas are less scared of losing control, of not being able to do something new thrown at us." He paused again. "And Moro really has stepped forward. I have always respected him. But what he is doing now . . ."

Nadia almost laughed. "Did you say, 'Betas scared'? You all act as if nothing ever scares you."

Nicholas smiled ever so slightly. "Yes, but that comes with the job. You are expected always to act fearlessly."

After the clan's population had shrunk to one hundred and ten during the crisis, the group hit two hundred members a year later and continued to grow—both innovating for the future and functioning well each day. Although only some of the rovers who had joined the clan had any basis for even speculating, some guessed correctly from their roving experiences that there was nothing quite like this clan, which melded Kat-management and Lena-like leadership, in the broader Meerkat world. They were pioneers.

Although it was never talked about officially, it came to be widely expected within the clan that the next set of Alphas might be either Nadia and Nicholas or Nadia and the new Head of Burrows: Ayo. Nadia secretly loved the idea, not for the status it would give her (well, maybe a bit for the status) but for the great privilege she would then have to further help build a great clan.

As the word began to spread about this clan, as it inevitably did through rovers, reactions started with disbelief, then a bit of jealousy, then growing admiration. And this admiration only continued to grow as the clan kept expanding while also handling well a Kalahari habitat that kept throwing new challenges at them.

It truly was a marvel to see.

The End.
(Well, almost.)

Some Thoughts About the Rise and Fall (and Re-rise) of Organizations

Unless you simply dislike fables for adults—in which case let us say we are extremely impressed that you had the discipline to make it past page 10—your mind has already been thinking about what here reminds you of your real-life experiences; what lessons there may be for you, your employer, or your school; what you might do to use this as a tool to alter your agenda or engage others in meaningful conversations about how to produce results your team very much wants and your organization very much needs; and, quite possibly, about many practical questions, especially if you have not seen anything like this succeed before. If you have enough ideas, or just want to think awhile, you may be done. Forget the rest of the book. Go think. And then act. If you have more questions than answers, want some answers, and like traditional business or professional books, you should read on.

Reviews from early readers have reported that our tale can provoke thought in a wide range of different areas: adapting to a changing environment, the challenges of getting bigger with the complexities that come with size, teamwork even among people in different silos or generations, creating an environment of openness to new and innovative ideas, becoming a continuous learning organization, dealing with adversity, learning to lead, and understanding the difference between leadership and management—to name only a few. But in closing, we would like to direct your attention to a few points that we think are particularly important in order to navigate yourself and others through a complex world with an increasing speed of change and with more disruptions to our business, public, and family habitats. These are a few points that we're convinced are at the core today of rising, falling, and the possibility of re-rising.

Leadership and Management

The most fundamental of the many issues here has to do with the nature of what we call "management," the nature of "leadership," and what they each accomplish when done well.

If you talk to enough people, you will find, as we have, many different and often contradictory answers to questions about management and leadership. The two words are often used interchangeably, suggesting that they mean roughly the same thing. They do not.

Management and leadership are *very* different in terms of actions, processes, and behavior. A one-page authentic and compelling vision that helps us see the direction in which we need to be moving is far from a thorough and thoughtful hundred-page (or five-hundred-page) operating plan. A carefully crafted process of inclusion and communication that helps to create a passionate group wanting to be a part of the journey and wanting to move in some direction is vastly different from an execution plan with budgets, organization charts, job descriptions,

Management	Leadership
· Planning · Budgeting · Organizing · Staffing · Measuring · Problem Solving · Doing what we know how to do exceptionally well in order to produce reliable, efficient results constantly.	· Establishing Direction · Aligning People · Motivating · Inspiring · Mobilizing people to see opportunities, overcome barriers, and leap quickly, agilely, and innovatively into a prosperous future.

and a focus on the right "skill sets" to do the job. Inspiring and encouraging people, touching their hearts and minds, and creating energy to overcome frustrating obstacles is very different from measuring results and rewarding or punishing people based on the metrics.

We are just as often told that leadership is related entirely to hierarchy level: Leadership is what the Alphas do and management is what the Betas do. But is it not true today that "Older Sisters and Brothers" who are much lower in a hierarchy than the Betas sometimes provide excellent leadership in their areas, to the benefit of all? And don't most of us have real-life examples of Alphas who no one thinks provide much leadership? In a similar sense, how often have we been told that leadership is only about what larger-than-life figures do? Even if we know that that cannot be entirely true, what effect do you think it has on us when such a message is repeated many times year after year after year?

Also, some people have been saying for at least the past few decades that leadership is increasingly needed and good, and should replace management, which is inherently clunky, bureaucratic, and command-control. But what happens with size and complexity if management is missing—as with Lena's clan?

Management and leadership serve different functions: The first can get the regular work done well, reliably, and efficiently, even in exceptionally large and complex systems; the second can energize us, despite barriers, to innovate swiftly and propel us into a prosperous future, despite changing problems and opportunities. Management and leadership are not two ways to achieve the same end. They serve different ends, both of which are essential in complex organizations that operate in changing environments.

In a large organization in a protected world that changes little, good management is overwhelmingly important—and, in a way, sufficient. In a small organization, perhaps opening a new market niche in a world where tomorrow's challenges and opportunities can change greatly at any time, leadership is overwhelmingly the key issue. For anywhere else, which includes tens if not hundreds of thousands of organizations on our planet today, it is both: because of their size or complexity (demanding management), and because they can't hide from the incredible technological and other forces creating change (demanding leadership).

Management and leadership are not incompatible as partners in an enterprise, although it can sometimes seem that way. It is not a matter of having one "or" the other, because they are so different: one emphasizing control of the masses of people, for example, the other a reasonably high degree of freedom and choice among people who can come from any part of that mass. In an organization of some size, in a world that is moving with speed and disruptions, does success not demand "and also"? Without "and also," won't you inevitably succumb, at least to some degree, either to the failures of the original Nicholas/Nadia clan or of Lena's group?

And why can it not be "and also"? Why not have controls in a hierarchical structure driving a plan to get today's work done exceptionally well *and* a sizable degree of freedom within a network structure guided by a clear directional vision to help people innovate, remove obstacles, reduce frustrations, and move everyone as fast as possible into the future? Necessity being the mother of invention, we suspect that we will be learning a whole lot more about all this in the next few decades.

Here is another chart that can put these complex structures, behaviors, and events in perspective.

This simple chart deserves a careful examination.

Virtually all organizations tend to rise from nothing

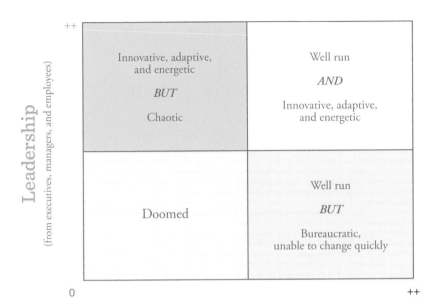

Leadership
(from executives, managers, and employees)

	++	
Innovative, adaptive, and energetic *BUT* Chaotic	Well run *AND* Innovative, adaptive, and energetic
Doomed	Well run *BUT* Bureaucratic, unable to change quickly

0   ++

Management
(from executives, managers, and employees)

by operating in the upper left quadrant. Those that soar move more often than not into the upper right, if only briefly, as they grow larger and larger. They escape the mind-set that kills change, the "we know how to do it, our success proves that." But the very elements they add to cope with increasing scale, the systems and structures and policies, all too easily kill off the Lena-like methods that create speed, agility, and innovation. And then organizations fall down into the lower right quadrant.

Those who do not have strong competitive pressures to deal with often solidify down there, becoming complacent, rigid, slow, and not the least bit strategically agile. When organizations are hit with sudden strong disruptions in their worlds, it can sometimes be as if the grid itself moves to the right, putting them in the lower left quadrant where they might be overwhelmed with what comes next and indeed be doomed.

Most mature organizations today appear to be somewhere in the lower right. In a slower-moving world they can perform well on some dimensions. But that sort of habitat is disappearing not only for our Meerkat friends but also for more and more of us everywhere.

Is the solution to this problem to go back to the leadership-driven, rapid-moving, low-rules, no-bosses, and innovative world of the upper left? For some this can be a tempting thought. But unless you are very small, is it not a naive thought? The solution is to rise again with a leadership-plus-management structure and processes that are represented by the upper right quadrant, where you do not subtract management but add a lot of leadership.

Another solution is to fight the pressures to ever move out of the upper left quadrant. This is understandable, especially if you are a brilliant leader/entrepreneur. But why would the result not always be the Lena scenario?

Creating a Best-of-Both-Worlds Organization

We are just now learning what it means to move into and remain in the upper right quadrant of our leadership/ management matrix. Many people are trying intuitively to do just that. In mature organizations, they are using leadership development education on far larger groups than in the past and making sure that the education is about leadership, not just management. They are adding new network-like groups (beyond traditional inter-departmental task forces) more aggressively and more creatively to their management systems. They are trying to engage the workforce more than in the past. They talk more about leadership and try explicitly to grow people as leaders. As we write this, we do not know the ideal way to move into the upper right quadrant of the matrix if you are a mature organization operating somewhere in the lower right quadrant. But we do know one way that can work, and it is what our Meerkat friends did.

The process is represented in the diagram shown below. It creates the sort of dual structure Nadia drew in

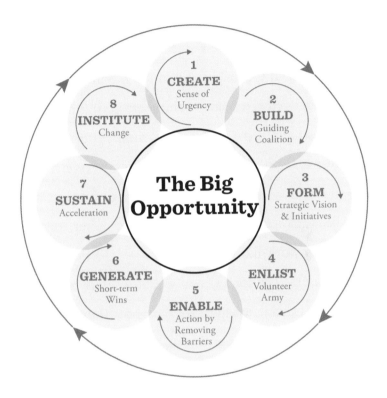

the sand and then makes it work to allow a high degree of management and leadership. It helps organizations beyond the start-up phase deal with efficiency and reliability to satisfy today's immediate demands despite size and complexity, as well as deal with a fast-changing world with all its demands for speed, agility, and innovation.

A dual system also has important auxiliary benefits that we are still learning about. For example, in today's war for talent, this system can attract and retain exceptional younger people who love the opportunity to take on broader (and more meaningful) assignments earlier in their careers.

Here is how it works:

1. The process begins by creating a high sense of urgency among large numbers of people around a clear big opportunity or opportunities. Complacency is driven down. A false sense of urgency that is produced by anxiety is driven down. Passion, excitement, and emotional engagement are driven up. Nadia and Nicholas did this with the help of a constantly growing group of others, especially Moro, through the relentless communication of exciting opportunities; through education;

through passion; and by offering evidence that pursuing new possibilites is feasible. It's the same as we have found in real organizations.

2. With real urgency around opportunity high, a very diverse group that spans across silos and at different levels is assembled, people who want so much to provide guiding and coordinating leadership in a new network-like system that they are essentially willing to do two jobs: their regular assignment in a hierarchy plus a second job in the leadership/innovation network. Again, think of a start-up, with young and old, engineers and sales types working together, arguing, and moving with a speed that seems incomprehensible in a big bureaucracy. In the real world, we have seen the Moros selecting this group or affirming someone else's selection of it, typically from a much larger group of volunteers who are passionate about taking on the new "night job."

3. This group, a guiding coalition of sorts, then acts like all great early-stage entrepreneurial units. It

develops initiatives that move it toward a vision that takes advantage of opportunities. It listens to voices everywhere, including from the Alphas and Betas, before choosing initiatives, and it rarely pursues any unless it can convince the Moros of the world that an idea has potential value.

4. There is relentless communication about the initiatives so that, with a high sense of urgency, enough volunteers to do the work will be drawn in. It is amazing, for example, what 5 percent of the people in an organization with five thousand employees can accomplish in a few months if you set up the conditions correctly. We have watched this again and again.

5. Much of what people accomplish is often less in inventing totally new ideas than in finding ones already sitting unseen by others (like our Meerkat's cuddly creature that led to the healing initiative), or taking ideas that are struggling to be implemented and knocking down barriers to actually executing them.

6. Successes—made, communicated, and celebrated—create change and develop momentum. In general, we have found, the more "wins" there are, even if small, the sooner they come, the more effectively they are communicated, and the more they are celebrated, the better.

7. With enough wins, attention is given to not letting urgency drop, selecting new strategically important initiatives, and keeping all of the processes going permanently.

8. And at some point big wins are institutionalized in the hierarchical structure, just like bug farming for the Meerkats became a new farming department with a boss and staff. With real results, volunteers will want to turn them over to others and the Alphas will want them sustained in the hierarchy to assure reliability and efficiency.

Much of this was discovered by one of us—Kotter—years ago. But today, in a faster-moving world, the basic method has grown and evolved in three particularly important ways. First, it is no longer a set of processes you bring out of the file drawer once every five, ten, or fifteen years. In a world that is changing more and more, faster and faster, the processes, once started, need to run continuously. Second, it requires many more people than before engaged not just in cooperating to implement the visionary ideas of top management but in finding ideas, dealing with all the institutional and attitudinal barriers to change, and motivating large groups to act in new ways—in other words, helping to lead. And third, to make the first two points practically feasible, it requires a second component working hand in glove with a traditional management-driven hierarchy, something that looks more like a highly successful start-up organization. And the very processes described above do just this despite the fact that mature organizations have a built-in tendency to kill off or marginalize anything that looks like a more egalitarian, fluid, innovative, and fast entrepreneurial structure.

But how is it realistically possible to create, in a sense, the best of both worlds, one of which has reliability and efficiency while the other offers agility, speed, and innovation? First and foremost, the processes, when introduced as described above, can overwhelm the many sources of resistance built into managerial hierarchies that just naturally kill off or limit the development and use of entrepreneurial, leadership-driven networks. The processes can overcome the incredibly powerful mantra of "that's not how we do it here." True urgency among large numbers of people around a real opportunity, that is not only seen intellectually but felt emotionally, is key. Education also helps, especially at the level of Betas and Alphas. But wins that demonstrate the viability and strength of a different system are essential; inspired action through words alone is always limited, especially when you are dealing with the new and uncertain. This is what happened in our Meerkat world, and we have seen it again and again recently in our human world.

If you, like the vast majority of us, have spent your life in lower-right-quadrant organizations, you may have dozens of questions that would require a few hundred more pages to answer. And that would obviously kill the virtues of a short book. But we do have two resources for you: a book in a traditional professional form titled *Accelerate* (by Kotter) and a wealth of material on the Kotter International Web site.

Here is another suggestion for a way to dig into these ideas in more depth. *Do not* put this book on your bookshelf. Pass it around and then use it as a basis for conversations about your department or office or division or firm. Readers of drafts of this manuscript have passed around a copy before already scheduled meetings (the yearly strategic planning session) or in advance of specially set sessions (a group of ten over a long lunch). Discussions seem to take their own natural form, starting with comments about our Meerkat story, then meandering onto talk about the organization at hand. Where are we in the two-by-two matrix? Why there? What are the consequences? Are there specific challenges we are not handling well or opportunities we are missing because of how we operate? Have we tried to change? What has worked and what has not? What are our biggest opportunities? And so on . . .

We have been hammered with ideas about control, project charters, task forces, boss-subordinate structures, metrics, and the like, usually for our entire careers. Under the circumstances, we naturally fear "throwing away" what we know. But that is not what we have been addressing here. It is addition, not subtraction. Giving in to this natural fear as we face new and more frequent strategic challenges will not serve us well.

With growing urgency around an opportunity, instruction, support from the top, momentum building because of initiative successes, and a hand-in-glove way of operating between two very different systems, it is possible to do as the Meerkats have done. We have seen successes up close, many times.

And yes, it can be amazing.

The Authors

John Kotter is an award-winning Harvard Business School emeritus professor of leadership, a *New York Times* bestselling author, a well-known business thought leader, and a cofounder of the Seattle- and Boston-based Kotter International.

Holger Rathgeber is a former executive with a global medical products corporation, a coauthor with Kotter of the international bestselling *Our Iceberg Is Melting*, and a principal at Kotter International.

Kotter International is a new breed of consulting firm that unlocks the full power of organizations to achieve strategic, sustainable results faster than leaders believe possible. It also helps leaders build sustainable organizations that are fast and agile as well as reliable and efficient. If you have enjoyed this book, we hope you will visit us at **www.kotterinternational.com**.

Have a Question?

Ask.

John.Kotter@KotterInternational.com

The End.

(For real, this time.)

If you loved *That's Not How We Do It Here!*, you'll also love . . .

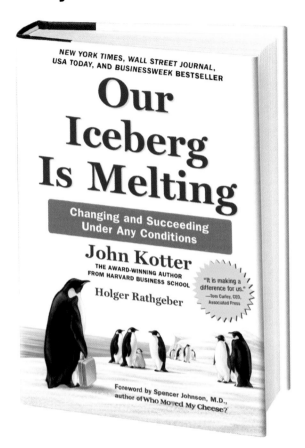

NEW YORK TIMES, WALL STREET JOURNAL, USA TODAY, AND BUSINESSWEEK BESTSELLER

Our Iceberg Is Melting

Changing and Succeeding Under Any Conditions

John Kotter
THE AWARD-WINNING AUTHOR FROM HARVARD BUSINESS SCHOOL

Holger Rathgeber

"It is making a difference for us."
—Tom Curley, CEO, Associated Press

Foreword by Spencer Johnson, M.D., author of *Who Moved My Cheese?*

"Everyone from CEOs to high school students can gain from what they take from this story." **—From the foreword by Spencer Johnson, M.D., author of *Who Moved My Cheese?***

"Companies should buy a copy for everyone from the CEO to the stock clerk." **—*USA Today***

"*Our Iceberg Is Melting* is superb. It embodies powerful messages that can help a broad audience. It covers all the steps to success in a changing world." **—Chris Hand, Citigroup**

PORTFOLIO PENGUIN
ISBN 9780399563911
www.kotterinternational.com/books

ry
Community Coll